# Saved by LOVE

# Saved by LOVE

**AN INCOMPLETE MEMOIR**

gloria fern

Copyright © 2020 gloria nafziger

All rights reserved. No part of this publication may be reproduced or transmitted in any form or by any means, electronic or mechanical, including photocopying, recording, or any information storage and retrieval system, without permission in writing from the author.

Published in 2020 by
Kinetics Design, KDbooks.ca
ISBN 978-1-988360-46-1 (paperback)
ISBN 978-1-988360-47-8 (ebook)

Front cover paintings: Z Heart and Z Strangely Quiet courtesy of Andrea Rinaldo, Butter Gallery, buttergallery.ca

Cover and interior design, typesetting and printing by Daniel Crack, Kinetics Design, KDbooks.ca, www.linkedin.com/in/kdbooks/

Contact the author at gfern52@gmail.com

*Dedicated to*

*Lora, Lisa and Kaitlyn*

*Love is everything.*

*And that is all we know about it.*

— EMILY DICKINSON

# Saved by LOVE

*Mine is a story of secrets.*

A story of chosen privacy in what at times felt like impossible pain.

A story of mothers and daughters. A story of change and growth. A story of unconventional love.

Mine is a story that offers hope, that reveals the surprising outcomes of self-love. In the theological language of my childhood, mine is a salvation story — born of the desire for wholeness in a patriarchal world of limited options and maximum control.

Saved by Love is the story of daring to leave the safe world of convention. Of knowing that I had to leave, because if I didn't I would die.

The story that begins in a mulberry tree beside a sap-dripping maple takes the reader on a journey from early marriage to a good man who would be a good father to the children I knew we would share, to leaving to save myself — learning how to honour the me I had long suppressed.

Readers of Saved by Love journey from the tight-knit world of East Zorra Mennonite Church, near Shakespeare, Ontario, home to a life of privilege and isolation, through scenes of hope and despair, and unexpected healing. Through marriage, divorce, coming out, the death of a partner and community activism, the journey that begins in Ontario's agrarian south ends near the great open waters of Georgian Bay, where I now live with my two partners.

*Z Strangely Quiet*

— ANDREA RINALDO

*This is a memoir, a historical account.*
*Some names have been changed.*

*A collection of memories, my memories.*

*I am telling a story of my life.*

*This book does not speak to the lives of any other persons mentioned here.*

*It does not speak to who those people are, or how they have experienced me.*

*I have written this memoir because the call of my soul was to write and share this story.*

*This is my story of the healing power of love.*

If you know me or anything about me, you will know I ramble, and my life rambles from one tale to the next, then back again, in reflection. So of course this is how I wrote these stories of my life, or a part of my life. The part about hope, about preservation and salvation.

As I attempt to find an order to my stories so that you, my readers, will understand, will be able to follow the tales and the wanderer, I start thinking about preserves lined on my mother's fruit cellar shelves. Even when I canned a lot, my shelves never held the bounty of my mother's shelves, which were carefully organized: sweets in one area, sours in another. I see beauty in the pink of the pears and plums, bright yellows in the mustard pickles and greens of the carefully sliced bread and butter pickles. There were peaches, beets, dills with little onions, and baby corns chosen carefully from the field, not too many or Dad would not be happy.

But then, how to categorize the times of despair ... which preserves represent bottled up despair?

So, I started over.

What about the labyrinth in my backyard, the cycling in and out of the flowers and the seasons? The bright yellow of daffodils, the red dahlias, the lilies magnificent, and the irises? All reminding me of Harriet's garden before she was too sick to care for it, before I helped her dig it up and moved it to my own garden. And then I felt my heart emerge — broken, wounded, bleeding — and you know by now I am sure that the heart moves back and forth from wounded to whole, from whole to fractured, from fractured to …

And cycles go on. So, as you read this incomplete memoir, my stories of preservation, of fractures and wholeness, of redemption and condemnation of the many cycles of my life, I invite you to find your story, your own assembling and falling apart, your own life's natural order.

*Twin Brooks Farm 1959*

On Twins Brooks Farm in 1959 the sun shines through the branches of the mulberry tree into my bedroom window. Wide awake, pulling my red plaid dress over my head, I race down the stairs, quilt bumping along behind. On the way to my sanctuary I check the sap pail on the maple tree shading the well, maybe Mom will say we can boil some today. I take one fingerdip taste, just enough to taste spring.

The mulberries were not even flowers. Buds filled the tree. Spring runoff from the creek and morning bird song companioned me as I lay against my friend, cozily wrapped in my patchwork quilt. I sat for a time almost falling back to sleep, hearing the sounds of the milking machines in the barn. It was Saturday — too soon I would be called to help with the baking and cleaning, but for now it was my morning. I threw down the quilt to climb into the sun-kissed tree. From there I could see small pieces of ice still standing strong on the field beside the lane. Most of the water was gone, running with so much other water across the laneway, over and under the bridge. Skating was over for this year, soon the water would recede and it would be time for boat-making, dam-building and, of course picking off blood suckers. For today I just needed to stay away from the water if I wanted to be outdoors, so away from the water I stayed, watching it rush by from my perch in the tree.

I saw Mom on her way in from the barn to make breakfast and called out,

"Can we boil sap today?" Her yes in response to me, had me running after her shouting. "Can we make pancakes too?"

Fall has come, the harvest is complete. The chickens are dancing headless, not yet scorched for feather removal. Soon, after the boiling-watered-chickens have cooled enough for me to touch, I will have to end my wanderings, sit on the stool and pull out feathers, being sure to get all the small pin feathers, "You do not want to eat those in your Thanksgiving dinner, do you?" Mom will say. I do not want to eat the pin feathers, but I do want to run and swing and slide on the set my father welded with love. I want to play with my cousin friends.

Butchering chickens is not as hard work as butchering pork and beef.

Grandpa is dead so the animals are no longer butchered on the farm. Dad has gone early, right after milking to pick up the slaughtered pigs at the butcher shop in North Easthope. Mom and Grandma got the fire boiling around the kettle stove, and I am awake for the excitement of the day and to be sure to not miss the first taste of crackle.

It is my job to take the pig brains to our neighbour Mel. Mom says he likes to eat them fried. Gross, I think, Mom thinks so too. I carry the container with brains very carefully down the lane and across the street. I knock on the door, Katie answers. Mel is in the barn. She says he could have come and got them himself. I say it is okay, Mom wanted to bring them over. Later, Mel comes across the road to thank us for his special treat. Mom's face gets all twisted up. Everyone laughs.

Dad is the sausage maker. I help wash the casings and put them in clean water to take to Dad, who is all set up with the sausage grinder that is visiting us for this, our butcher day. Dad's finger does not get cut off in the sausage grinder on this day. That happened long before I was born, when he was a little boy, I guess he was the sausage maker then too.

Mom tells him to be careful, not to be so *sushlich*.

No one will tell me if they ate the sausage that his finger was in.

When I ask, they all look at one another, but do not answer.

My aunts and uncles and cousins go home.

The excitement of the day is over.

The butcher work will not be done for a long time. We will have to cut up sausage into little pieces. Grandma will chop, she is afraid I will cut myself but I will not, I can be careful! My job will be to shove the pieces into the jar, way down to the bottom and push the pieces tightly together. Sometimes I put the salt on the top before the lids go on and the jars are plunged into the steamer. Then the kettle stove needs to be washed, if it is cool enough, along with the knives and the aprons and bowls and the tables that have been made for this occasion, our pig-butchering days.

I am always surprised when the jars come out of the steamer and the meat is swimming juice and lots of white lard.

I wonder where it came from.

Life for me is like that, full of wonder.

*Collingwood 2019*

Sitting at my desk in Collingwood, watching the birds and blooms dance in the labyrinth, the long braids are long gone now and my short hair is greying. I am a grandmother, a partner, a sister, a friend, a lover, a writer, a gardener, a walker, a reader, a mother. I look in the mirror and see my mother's dark brown eyes, surrounded by life lines, looking out at me.

I am living in a small town near the water and great hiking trails. I love to swim in the bay and hike on the trails. I am planning a walking trip to Spain.

I sometimes eat sausage but rarely do I find any as good as my father's was, the perfect mix of salt pepper and other spices, never any garlic — my mother disliked it so!

I eat a lot of garlic.

I do not butcher chickens. I buy pin feather-almost-all-plucked hormone-free chickens from our local butcher or at the farmers' market. Our vegetable garden is small. I garden for pleasure, not necessity. My gardening delight is the perennial floral labyrinth in the backyard, in bloom from early spring to late fall. The snowdrops are blooming now, and even a dainty purple primula is showing its head. I must rake carefully so as not to knock off their heads. The grasses that grow around it need excavation constantly and when time and desire blend, I excavate.

I am accompanied in my life.

My dear friend Harriet who, before she died promised me visits, visits often. My mother and Bonnie also join me in the beauty of the bird song and the blooms. It delights me that these three souls are connected on the other side.

In the centre of the labyrinth I sit, wishing I had brought my journal.

I live a life of wonder, a life of great privilege, abundant love.

Hard to believe from this vantage point that there were days when suicide seemed the only way ahead.

*Brunner, Ontario 1988*

The bedroom that Ron and I share has two windows, including one above the headboard. The quilt that covered our bed in the moment that the yellow bird called to me, to my sobbing head buried in the pillow, was purple and white, given to us as a wedding present from the mother of my best friend in college. Kathy's family lived in Pennsylvania.

Could the yellow bird see purple through the window?

The first time I heard the tap tap tapping, I looked for a downy woodpecker in the large maple between our house and Ron's aunt and uncle's home, only there was no red head and black and white body. There was a yellow bird that looked like a canary, on our window sill. It was tapping on the glass on the window. Tapping like it wanted to come in.

It was a bright yellow bird, and it was free, and it came three days in row. Yes, it is true. I was laying on the bed for three days in a row. The bird came every day.

*Twin Brooks Farm 1970*

My family home was often the site of Saturday night youth parties that included youth from as many as five churches, up to 50 or more young people milled around our large farm kitchen. Board and card games were played on the floor and tables. There was always food, some salty and some good home baking. Fred and Wilbur were always delighted when my mother (or I ) made pie. Pop Shoppe was available in a variety of flavours, black cherry a favourite. Laughter and music filled the kitchen, dining and living room of our yellow brick farmhouse.

No matter how late the party went, Dad, Mom and my oldest brother Dale would be up and in the barn by 6 a.m. to begin the daily chores. Feeding, milking, cleaning. I sometimes went too, but usually my work was in the house. When I wanted to invite friends over from school or the community — friends who not a part of church — there was never any question, friends were welcomed.

My mother never once questioned my choice of friends or the value of them in my life. She delighted in me having friends. I believe she didn't want me ever to be alone or isolated.

*August 2007, Tavistock*

I am visiting my mother, we are cutting corn off the cob and freezing it for the winter. Mom and Dad are no longer living on the farm, they have retired into town and my brother Kevin and his wife Carolyn have bought the farm. Since there is no longer sweet corn planted in the fields on the farm, the corn comes from my aunt Arlene, who lives with my uncle, Dad's younger brother, on the farm that I used to go to visit grandma and grandpa Kropf.

We are chatting in the back yard, knives in hand, bowls in our lap.

My mother has stopped cutting, she is looking at me.

"Is Susan moving to England?"

Surprised, I say, "No," wondering at the question.

"Oh," she says. "Reta said she was."

"Rachel, Susan's daughter, is going to school in London," I reply. We had discussed Rachel's plans in our visit with Reta, a couple of days before.

"Oh, that is good," says Mom. "Is Susan moving to Collingwood with you and Liw?"

"Yes, yes she is," I take a deep breath, waiting.

"I am glad," says my mother, "but Collingwood, is so far away."

"Don't worry, I will visit," I say.

"I hope so," her too-soon answer.

"And" I say, " it is beautiful there, you will come up too."

A slight pause and then it came, her quiet response "Maybe."


### *Waterloo Oxford High School 1972*

As a teenager, I wondered if I was like all other teenagers who were brought up with Old and New Testament stories. Maybe all their nightmares included being smothered in granaires filled with wheat.

The story of Joseph and his multi-coloured dream coat was not an unfamiliar story at Waterloo Oxford District Secondary School, especially not in my ISCF (Interschool Christian Fellowship) group. Students from a variety of churches — Pentecostal, Missionary, Brethren, Mennonite — talked about what we knew about living a life as a Christian in a secular world. Maybe I was like all other Christian teenagers. But we did not discuss, in ISCF or MYF (Mennonite Youth Fellowship) waking up in a cold sweat, feeling like we were suffocating.

I do not remember being a member of any group conversations that began:

"I was thinking of killing myself."

"Me too."

"Life is really hard."

I remember that if anyone even hinted in that direction, the conversation was redirected. Reminders that God loves you and doesn't make junk.

Reminders to have faith. Reminders that nothing can separate us from God's love, except for lack of faith, and our own failure.

When I found the note in my locker in the early days of grade 9, I did not tell anyone. Or maybe I told my cousin Brenda. Some anonymous person told me I stunk, that no one wanted to be my friend. I knew I had only given my locker combination to one girl, who went to my church. I did not tell the ISCF or my church youth group that I was afraid there was something very wrong with me.

I hated that my period started and blood got on my blue Crimplene dress that my mom had made. I was ashamed.

### East Zorra Mennonite Church 1974

I got married at East Zorra Mennonite church in 1974, I was 19.

I knew what I wanted.

I wanted to be a good wife, a happy wife.

I did not want to be rebellious. I did not mean to be.

I did have a lot of questions, I always had lots of questions.

My cousin Brenda and her sister Carol were frequent sounding boards.

Why did my husband Ron and his friends get to play hockey in the winter and baseball in the summer and no one questioned whether they were good fathers or husbands?

Why, when I was involved in anything outside the home, did people question my mothering?

Why, when God was referred to as a mother hen in the Bible was it a big deal for me to identify God as female?

Why, when I went away, and left the children with Ron, was he "babysitting" and not parenting?

They did not laugh at my questions. Brenda and Carol listened and sometimes shared the same questions. Brenda sometimes said, gently, "It does not matter …." Or "You try too hard."

I did not know how to fit in like she did. I wished I could.

Ron laughed at my questions. He questioned if I would ever be truly happy, would I ever be content? Stop rocking the boat, he told me. He reminded me we live in a nice community, we have a good church, our families support and love us, we have lots of wonderful friends.

## Brunner 1987

I go to see the doctor, I am worried. I have a bad headache, a really bad headache, he says it is caused by stress. I tell the doctor I have a good marriage, wonderful children, we are foster parents, I have lots of support. He says, take these pills. He says, if your headache goes away, we know it is anxiety, if it does not I will order a CT scan. I am frustrated. He does not listen to me, but I will not break down in his office.

I agree to take the pills.

My headache goes away.

I find a therapist.

I analyze with therapists.

The window frame, the window, the bird, the colour, the headaches.

I do not know how to free myself from this world that is mine, that is supposed to be good, that I should be grateful for.

I could feel God's love through the headaches.

I know God's love and I know God's call on me: to love.

I tell our foster daughter, after her release from jail, that I would like it if she came to church with me.

"Gloria," she says, "I cannot ever be good enough for those people. I am not good enough for your church."

I say, "You are good enough."

She says, "I smoke."

I laugh. "You only need to change what God asks you to change, you are a perfect child of God." I do not believe in a love of restriction. I know we need to love and to accept all people.

I tell her all of this but she is still afraid of judgment.

### *Milverton Mennonite Church 1988*

I argue with our minister, my friend, about the couple at Milverton Mennonite Church who are not married. I do not agree with the elders, that the two should live in separate homes until their divorces are complete. The elders cannot decide who the children should live with. I talk about our choice — to live by love, instead of law. I believe that living by love is greater than fear.

I am afraid.

The Mennonite Church grew out of the Anabaptist Reformation. I learned about the Reformation and the martyrs who died because of their faith, as a child. I grew up knowing that the Mennonite church was the true church. The Mennonite Confession of Faith, on which congregational life is based, has 24 articles. Article 19 is about marriage and states: God intends marriage to be a covenant between one man and one woman for life. Article 18 article is entitled "Spirituality." The last paragraph says, "we are convinced that nothing can separate us from the love of God in Christ Jesus our Lord."

There is no pope in the Mennonite Church — ostensibly, a non-hierarchical church (that may be debatable but it is not the theme of this story), meaning that the interpretation of scripture and even the understanding of the Confession of Faith varies from congregation to congregation.

## Dew Drop Inn Stratford 1973

Fred and Brenda were 19 and I, 18, when we got jobs at the Dew Drop Inn, a coffee shop and youth hostel housed in the old YMCA. The cafe was run by Grace Brunk. Grace was, according to my mother, a holy roller, she and her husband had left the Mennonite church and were involved in some cult-like group, my mother said.

My mother did not want me to be too close to Grace. She was not from one of the inside families within the Mennonite world, this much I knew.

Grace intrigued me. Grace seemed happy.

She was interesting, curious and appeared to be non-judgemental. I never heard her complain about how others treated her, she did not talk about not belonging in the world where she grew up.

She challenged me to listen and learn and be curious about life. She talked about the Holy Spirit and how She could be a guide in my life. The Holy Spirit was a part of the Trinity, there was God, the father, Jesus Christ his only Son, and the Holy Spirit. I was surprised to learn from Grace that the Holy Spirit was a She.

I was excited to work with two of my best friends for the summer. To share adventures and to truly belong. We were to be Christian witnesses especially for people who did not know Christ, and who lived in a world of drugs and sin.

The only people who were not normal, that I knew in Stratford, were associated with the Shakespearean festival, mostly actors and musicians. They lived in a world different from the Mennonite Christian world I lived in. At the Dew Drop Inn, in the summer of my 19th year, I met Steven. I knew Steven spent time with some of the actors.

Steven said he liked men. Steven said he was a woman.

Steven said he was born into the wrong body. He felt like a woman, in a man's body. He explained he was not gay.

My biggest concern about Steven was that he smoked.

I liked him and did not want him to get cancer, and I knew that smoking was bad. I used to steal his cigarettes (for his own good) to try and get him to quit. One day Fred and I took Steven's pack of cigarettes and poked holes in them so he could not smoke them. Steven was furious and told me in no uncertain terms that I was being arrogant in thinking I knew what God or anyone else wanted him to do, or in believing that I knew what was better for him than he did.

Steven and I became friends, sharing our hopes and our fears.

I wanted someone to want me, I wanted to be loved.

He wanted to be a woman. I did not understand wanting to be a woman, but I did feel his pain at not belonging in the world, and not being seen as who he truly was. We shared our deep soul longings. Being a Jesus Freak did not mean you did not care about others who were suffering. It was not so different from being a hippie, you just got high on Jesus instead of drugs, and that was a good thing.

I begin dating Ron, go away to Eastern Mennonite College in Harrisonburg Virginia and lose touch with Steven.

When I come home after my school year away, Ron proposes to me in the living room at my parents' house. He has just come home from a trip to Europe.

"Will you marry me?"

"Are you kidding? You want to marry me?"

He says he is not kidding and yes, he does want to marry me.

I look at him. "Okay," I say, "But Kathy comes along with the deal."

He laughs. Ron says, "Sure, I know she is like a sister to you."

Kathy is my best friend from college who lives in Pennsylvania. She laughs when I tell her, says she likes Ron, and is glad we will still visit lots.

## Cassel 1974

Ron and I go to a house party. August. We have been engaged 3 months.

I meet a young woman at the party. "Gloria," she says, "don't you remember me?"

I look at her eyes and see. "Steven, are you in there?"

Steven — now Stephanie — laughs at my discomfort and shares with me what it feels like to be living congruently.

The trees under which we stand seem to clap their hands.

As Ron drove me home into the darkness of the night, I share with him my experience of talking with Stephanie.

Ron questions Steven's spiritual well-being.

I am silent.

I marry Ron in November.

*Twin Creeks Farm 1969*

Grandma visited me soon after she died. It was the first time that someone dead visited me. She sat on the end of my bed and looked at me and said, it will all be all right. She told me it was good for me to be me, that life would be all right and she would still watch out for me. When I told Mom all this, she said I'd had a dream.

It was a good dream. I was 15 years old.

*Brunner 1991*

I was trying to be happy. It was New Year's day. I was not sure that life would be all right

The carol singing, the Christmas Eve service, the visiting after, had all gone well. Today was the beginning of a wonderful new year of hope and possibility, the year of the sheep, according to the Chinese zodiac which we read in the Chinese restaurant. A year of gentle calm. I did not feel the gentle calm, although I wanted it.

I put the dirty dishes from the previous day's gathering with Ron's family into the dryer, I was not doing laundry, and no one would bother to look there. I just needed the place to look clean.

I did not have time to make the house look better than I felt, and I needed it to look nice. I put on some of my favourite clothes. I put on makeup. Friends from church were coming again, to play games and to celebrate the new year.

The house filled with laughter, games and chatter. Carols played quietly in the background.

I felt alone.

No one knew me, no one knew my struggle, except maybe Cheryl, who with Linda had gone to visit family for a couple weeks.

I could not talk to Cheryl. I could not hear her reassurance, I could not listen while she told me it would all be okay. I could not visit her at the apartment she had moved into the week before Christmas and share a cup of tea or a glass of wine.

Chris was my other option, but she and Jack were gone. They had headed off to visit family too. I could not remember where they were, I thought in Toronto with Jack's family but perhaps they were still in Minnesota, the land of Chris's childhood. Oh, how I wished either Chris or Cheryl were home.

I went to check on my daughters, the ones who convinced me that life was worth living. Lora was busy playing games, and Kaitlyn and the plethora of little girls her age that filled our church and her life were completely oblivious to my entry as they delighted in the pet town that was Kaitlyn's Christmas present this year. Lisa, as so often happened in a crowd, was also happy in her own world, curled up with a book on her bed. The book engulfed her, my greeting went completely unnoticed.

They did not need to keep me alive.

I could do it. A part of me hoped I could.

My mother began her life in 1930, as the youngest of six children, the beloved baby girl, whose mother almost died from hemorrhage giving birth. I began my life in 1954, I was the daughter, the second-born child in a family of five children, whose mother almost died from hemorrhage giving birth to me. I have three daughters, none of whose mother almost died when they were born. I knew the name of the youngest before she was conceived.

Perhaps I knew all three of my daughters before they were born. I knew that I would give birth to daughters, I knew the love that I felt for them before they were born, before I married their father, I knew them.

I know the story of the woman who had been bleeding, who had a blood disease. I learned it on my grandmother's knee. Matthew, chapter 9. The woman's story is a story about faith.

Faith, the substance of things hoped for, the evidence of things not seen. Hebrews 11 verse 1. It says all this in the Good Book, as my father called the Bible when he told me I should not be reading other books.

The crowd in the house was still playing games, the dishes were still in the dryer and I needed to talk to someone. I mustered all the faith I could find and went into the office. I dug out my notes from the Multiple Personality Disorder course I was taking in Stratford as a part of my continuing education and found Marie Louise's phone number. I dialed the phone, wondering if I was breeching professional boundaries.

I did not care. I closed the door.

"I do not know if you remember me," I began tentatively.

"I am taking your course in Stratford."

It was New Year's day. A holiday, I continued talking.

"I think you are a lesbian, are you a lesbian? I need help."

There was silence. "I am in a relationship with a woman," Marie Louise said.

"Are you a Christian," I asked?

Another affirmative answer.

"Can you talk to me?"

Her reassuring voice offered some comfort. She, unlike Cheryl, had not been kicked out of a Christian college for being a lesbian, she had been excommunicated from a church.

She told me her story. She talked about how important the church had been and still was to her, how hard it was to lose friends and community because of who she loved. How wonderful it was to love. She said her children had gone to a Christian school. She talked about the power of the Spirit in her life, and how the Spirit was leading her. She talked about her understanding of the connection between spirituality and sexuality.

Yes, her children struggled. "Children," she said, "do not want to have to think about their mother's sexuality. Children want their mothers to have it all figured out. They do not," she said, "want to see their mothers hurt by people they love."

I would protect my children, I thought as she talked. I listened, trying to hold onto the words so they would not disappear from my grip.

She promised me we could get together after the next class, a couple of weeks from now. She hung up after I promised not to hurt myself before then.

What supports did I have nearby? Who could I call?

I missed my church friends.

I had not believed Chris when she told me they would not support me if I came out.

I should have listened.

Holly was in Nova Scotia for Christmas with Jerry and their girls, visiting her family. I called her to go for a walk as soon as she returned. As a musician at the Stratford Festival, she must know LGBT people. I thought she would hear me.

I had not told her about my emerging awareness.

I was grateful that Holly rented a home outside of Stratford, near me, I was grateful that she was not a church friend, that she was a neighbourhood friend. I could talk to her about anything. Holly was not afraid of difference.

We walked down the dirt road past leafless trees, plowed and stubbled fields, together we laughed and cried as we shared stories. She did not think that being attracted to women was a problem. I was grateful to be her friend, not a problem to solve.

I met Marie Louise at a workshop she was leading with Margo Rivera in Stratford. The course started in September and we met one weekend a month for eight months. Four weekend meetings had happened so far. I attended the workshop with my friend from church, Janine. We were two very different women who had great discussions that some would have called arguments. Cheryl attended the workshop as well. It was a workshop on Multiple Personality Disorder.

Marie Louise and Margo were great teachers and integrated spirituality heavily into their workshop. At some point during the training I was struck with the knowledge that these women were lesbian. They were deeply spiritual and lesbian. I was awestruck and delighted! On the drive back to my small town home in Brunner, I looked at my friend, Janine, who knew about my newly emerged sexual identity, and had said it was okay to be lesbian as long as I did not act on it. She said, "God would lead me through." We had many conversations on what exactly it meant to act on "IT."

I looked at Janine, my social work friend from church, as we drove home on that December day, and said to her,

I looked at Janine …, and said to her, "they are lesbian."

Janine looked at me surprised and asked, "Who? Who is lesbian?"

"Marie Louise and Margo."

"They are, "Janine replied," far too spiritual to be lesbians."

Janine then reminded me that it was okay to be a lesbian as long as I did not act on it. Then she reassured me of her and God's love for me.

I began attending Olive Branch Mennonite Church after Ron and I separated. I began attending when he promised he would fight me for custody if I did not take the girls to church, to a Mennonite Church.

There was no publicly affirming or welcoming Mennonite church for lesbian or gay people in 1991.

When Bonnie moved in with my daughters and me, she began to attend Olive Branch with us.

"If they are truly a social justice community," she said, they will accept us as a couple. Welcoming the outcast," she said, "is a part of the call of Jesus."

Bonnie had gone to a United Church in her earlier years. She did not know or care about the Mennonite edict to be the quiet in the land, and she was not going to be the quiet, silent nobody in this small congregation.

## Sharbot Lake 1993

Thirteen-year-old Lisa and I are paddling into the reeds, red-winged blackbirds, blue dragon flies flit around us. "Mom," Lisa says from the back of the canoe on this lake at this cottage, this visit a gift to us, in the midst of Bonnie's illness.

"Yes, honey."

"I was thinking, that since you are with a woman, then I can probably love whoever I love, right?"

We chuckle together as I acknowledge, "Yes, yes, that is probably true." And yes she is right that this might be a good thing to come out of my coming out.

## Kitchener 1991

My therapist knew a priest, the priest had a parishioner. The priest and the parishioner were both lesbian. The priest introduced me to her parishioner, whose name was Gretchen. I met her for the first time in Tim Horton's on Victoria Street in Kitchener. I walked in to find a stranger. There was a lot of walking in to find a lot of strangers in those days. It was this stranger who would accompany me to the Toronto Pride Parade in July. It was this friend who would accompany me to Holy Trinity Church before the Pride Parade. It was this courageous woman who would push me forward when I saw the BMC (Brethren Mennonite Council for Gay Lesbian Concerns) banner at Pride.

It was Gretchen who would say, of course you need to go talk to them. She was at the time a member of the Missouri Synod Lutheran church, although she was attending the Anglican church. She understood my attachment to the Mennonite church and community. We were both trying to sort out how we would remain married to the men we had vowed to be faithful to till death do us part.

I drove nervously, excitedly, to Toronto on the Sunday morning of the Pride Parade, and together we went to Holy Trinity Church, a church that Chris had introduced me to. I was surprised and amazed that this Anglican church was standing so near the Eaton Centre in Toronto and serving meals to all who came, because they stood up to the Eaton Corporation and refused to be bought out. The church served the unserved, the poor, in the midst of consumerism. I was delighted to be able to walk the labyrinth and sit with confidence in a service where I would not be judged for my orientation or gender. After sharing soup with others at the church, Gretchen and I headed over to Church Street, toward the Pride Parade.

We wandered in amazement through a brave new world, through the booths and the displays, where we came upon the BMC table. This was a table staffed by and for Mennonite and Brethren gays and lesbians.

I was both delighted and a little nervous to be at the parade. I was married, I was going to stay married. Someone might know me. The Mennonite world is small, I knew that, I had been Mennonite my whole life.

I had called the BMC office in Minnesota months before to seek support, anonymous support, and was given the name of a former minister (he had come out too), in Iowa. Within moments, Keith Schrag from Iowa had identified where I lived and that his cousin, lived on the street I had grown up on, and was a good friend of my mother's.

So I was not surprised when I chatted on Church Street with Greg Lichti to learn he knew people, in fact was related to people in Brunner, and as I asked him to maintain my confidentiality, around the corner came Bob Bender, who had sung with me in the CHET yf (Cassel, Hillcrest, East Zorra, Tavistock youth fellowship) choir. We looked at each other, shocked or surprised to see one another in this setting.

While I knew he was gay, it had never been discussed.

He broke the silence.

"Hi, Gloria." He continued, "I thought you were married to Ron? Don't you have children?"

"Yes, I am married to Ron. Yes, I do have three little girls."

"Do you and Ron go to Milverton Mennonite Church?"

Milverton was known by much of the Mennonite conference as a theologically conservative, evangelical congregation.

## Stratford General Hospital 1990

I sit, twirling my hair in the staff meeting at Stratford General hospital. I am on a placement for my masters of social work degree. I am in a staff meeting, the room is filled with hospital-beige paint, social workers and a psychologist. I smile as people enter. I take my hand away from my hair. I cross my legs. I am wearing new clothes, social worker clothes.

My heart leaps as I realize my life is unravelling, from the inside out.

The knots are no longer tight.

I have been tying knots for a long time.

Sometimes, consciously.

The nice, solid Mennonite man/boy I married in 1974, when I was almost 20, was 5 years older than me, a mechanic who worked at his family farm equipment business.

Before our first date, a double date, he told me he would take me out so that his friend Jim would be brave enough to ask out my friend Bonnie. I was grateful to go on a date. Finally, a boy who did not see me as one of the guys, a good Mennonite boy who wanted to take me on a date, not talk to me about all the girls he wanted to date. We went to see Cabaret.

The arrangements for our date were made a Saturday night earlier. Bonnie and Jim were flirting from across the room, he on one side, she on the other, of the white brick Victorian home I shared with my parents and brothers. My grandmother, now dead, no longer lived in the downstairs bedroom, beside the stairway and the living room. The rooms were all filled with teens. As always, we were laughing, playing games of Twister, Monopoly and Rook, eating salt and drinking Pop Shoppe.

Ron and I married 18 months after our first date, which was six months before I went away to Eastern Mennonite College (EMC) in Harrisonburg Virginia. Ron's mother worried about me getting pregnant before marriage, my mother worried about me not finishing school.

Ron and I were active in the church before and after our wedding day. I went with him to his church, it was closer, kind of, anyway. We were active on committees, taking leadership roles. I became a good Christian wife. I did not agree with the faith of some around me, I did not accept that women should be submissive to men. I did not accept that the order of things was God Man Woman Child.

I did believe in Jesus. I did believe in Salvation. I was grateful that Jesus gave his life, so that I (and you, if you believed) could have life everlasting. I shared my faith with others.

## *Brunner 1986*

We were foster parents, Ron and I. We also had three little girls. I loved being a mother. I was talking with our foster daughter's social worker. It was close to Christmas. She told me with a smile and twinkling eyes that they would have an interesting gathering for Christmas. She said there would be a Marxist, an atheist, and a Buddhist at their table, along with her and her husband.

I was not sure if she was a Christian or not, she went to an Anglican church. When she told me about all those who would be gathered at the table in 1986, I said, "Oh, so all those people will be gathering to celebrate the birth of our Lord and Saviour." A shadow washed across her face as she stammered, "Well, I guess so."

I tried not to miss opportunities to share the good news of Jesus with other people. I loved Jesus the radical, the one who accepted and supported people on the fringes of society.

I was pretty sure that Jesus loved me too, imperfect as I was.

We had a foster daughter living with us. I believed that I could heal her with God's help. I did not really believe that God was letting me down because I did not accept all the teachings of our church. I believed that if I prayed enough, this young woman would be able to accept the help I was offering and her self-harming behaviours would end. All I needed was more faith.

I thought, if I would just pray more, if I could trust more, my headaches would go away and she would be healed.

What was wrong with my faith?


I wished, I often wished, that I would like this person who was me, or I believed others liked the person that I was supposed to be. I was glad that Jesus loved me.


### Kitchener 1995

My Bible is sitting on the shelf, I take it down and open it. There were many notes written there. Notes from years past and not so many years past. That bible holds a history of me.

*Jesus is a Marxist*, I read on one of the pages, there is a happy face beside it. I read the underlined Beatitudes.

1 Now when Jesus saw the crowds, he went up on a mountainside and sat down. His disciples came to him

2 and he began to teach them. He said:

3 Blessed are the poor in spirit, for theirs is the kingdom of heaven.

4 Blessed are those who mourn, for they will be comforted.

5 Blessed are the meek, for they will inherit the earth.

6 Blessed are those who hunger and thirst for righteousness, for they will be filled.

7 Blessed are the merciful, for they will be shown mercy.

8 Blessed are the pure in heart, for they will see God.

9 Blessed are the peacemakers, for they will be called children of God.

10 Blessed are those who are persecuted because of righteousness, for theirs is the kingdom of heaven.

11 Blessed are you when people insult you, persecute you and falsely say all kinds of evil against you because of me.

12 Rejoice and be glad, because great is your reward in heaven, for in the same way they persecuted the prophets who were before you.

— MATTHEW 5

*God does not make junk*, is written there beside *suicide is not an option for a Christian*. Nothing, it says, in another underlined passage, nothing can separate you from God's love.

I wrote it in my Bible, I wrote it in my journals. God does not make junk.

I wanted to believe it was true. I wanted to believe.

*Brunner 1988*

I was not fond of me, I was moody, given to uncertainty around where my life was taking me.

My greatest happiness was brought by motherhood, of that there was no doubt. Motherhood had taken away the possibility of suicide. Most days.

I did not want to leave that legacy for my children and I was convinced that they would never know how truly depressed and discouraged I was by this seemingly perfect life.

## *Waterloo 1991*

When I graduated with my master's degree in 1991 my mother, smiling broadly said, "I am so happy to see this day." She made eye contact as she said this. "I did not think you would finish grade 11." I had achieved something she could only dream about. Not only had I been able to go to high school, I had completed college, then gone on to get a bachelor's degree. Now, a master's.

My mother, father, husband and three daughters sat through the ceremony, unaware, I believed, of the inner turmoil that accompanied me across the stage.

I was congratulated by a Mennonite classmate's mother. "Your grandmother was a saint, your mother is a saint, and now you are a saint just like them."

"Thank you," I replied, smile pasted in place.

*Kitchener 1993*

While Olive Branch discussed whether or not Bonnie and I could be members and while I travelled from church to church as exhibit number one, or three, or seven, a real lesbian, sometimes in the company of a real gay man or another lesbian, I read.

I read Melanie Morrison's *The Grace of Coming Home*, and came to know her as a dear friend. Melanie celebrated her lesbian and Christian identities, a foreign concept in most of my world. Bonnie and my attendance at our first Sisters in a Strange Land retreat, a retreat for Christian Lesbians connected me with a theology and women who validated my life and journey.

I read Carter Heyward's *Touching our Strength*. I read Sue Monk Kidd's *Dance of the Dissident Daughter*: "When a woman starts to disentangle herself from patriarchy, ultimately she is abandoned to her own self."

And when I read, and expanded my circle I found that I was not alone. I found as I sat in the old deep white-grey bathtub on Pandora Ave, with *Dance of the Dissident Daughter* just above water level, that writer after writer spoke to the importance of my stories being heard and witnessed.

I felt encouraged to keep telling my story, in the hopes of being validated. I was sometimes validated, but as I told the same stories over and over again in the church to often hostile listeners,

I also felt deep pain.

The nice man who had married me over 15 years before, who had become the father to my three amazing daughters, was getting more and more conservative in his world view. Sometimes I wondered if he was always that conservative and I had simply failed to notice. But he was a nice man, most of the time he was kind and supportive, though often absent, he was a busy man, and an important man who had a business to run and customers to care about.

When Ron and I were getting married, in 1974, my mother told me sometimes you have to give it to them even when you do not want to.

## Brunner 1989

I was so tired as I wailed out to God. I was trying hard to be all I believed God wanted me to be. I needed God's help. And he had replied, as she often replied again, Love is what matters.

Love.

"What is next?" I asked from my tear-stained pillow.

The voice responded clearly. "Homosexuality is next and all you need to remember is to love."

OK, I thought that is not so hard, I have loved others that the Church told me were unlovable, unwelcome, I can do this too.

So I accepted the invitation. I knew some homosexuals already and I loved them. I did. I was going to meet another homosexual and I was supposed to love them. I could do that.

I would do that.

*Kitchener 1991*

I went to see Gloria Taylor, a therapist who, according to other therapists, including the one I was seeing at the time, was the most informed about lesbians, in Kitchener. I had come to know Gloria through a family reconstruction class that she taught at the seminary. I had taken the course as an elective in my Social Work course. I had attended other courses that Gloria taught. Gloria and I knew each other through mutual friends and acquaintances. I was struggling. So I called her office.

When I walked in she said, "What do you want? Is this a professional or social meeting?"

I longed for small talk. She did not. I said, "I am trying to figure out if I am lesbian."

Gloria laughed. She had a full and hearty laugh. "Gloria," she asked, "have you ever had an orgasm?"

"I am not sure," I said, "maybe when my babies were born."

She looked at me compassionately. "Have you ever sneezed? she asked. "You would know," she said.

*Twin Brooks Farm 1960*

When my mother was pregnant with who would turn out to be my third brother, Kevin, she was bedridden. That is when Elsie came to work for us. Elsie was from Wellesley, she was our hired girl.

Elsie was a black-car Mennonite. The first time she came to our house, she came with her sisters, and her mother and father. I loved playing with her sisters in their flowing flowered dresses and coverings with strings. Elsie would just laugh when my father called her a tomboy. She didn't care. She taught me to ride two bikes at once, she climbed up the ladder and painted the very peak of our three-storey yellow brick farm house. Elsie was not afraid.

When my mother got pregnant with Larry, who I later dressed up in my old dresses, put him in the stroller and called Linda, Elsie came back. This time she usually came with Aaron. She did not teach me as many things then, and she was not as much of a tomboy. I missed the tomboy Elsie. I went to girls' club at church when mom was pregnant. We had fun at girls' club, even though we had to sew. I told one of the other girls that my mom was going to have a baby. She told me her mom was going to have a baby too. We were excited. When our moms, who had been good friends since their teen years, found out that we had talked about their growing bellies at girls' club, we were forbidden to go the next month.

I was confused, because soon everyone would know. But I did not talk about babies in bellies again for a very long time.

### *Steinman Mennonite Church 1993*

Fred and I sit in his office at Steinman Mennonite Church, where he is a minister. He wants to talk to me again. It has been years since we laughingly solved the world's problems until late into the night. Today we are not sharing our solutions, today we are not just talking, today he is challenging me, he is sharing his concern for me.

He is confronting me in love, according to Matthew 18:15. "If your brother or sister sins, go and point out their fault."

I tell him I need to be congruent, I want to live a life of congruence.

Fred says, "What is it with you people and congruence?"

I retort, "I actually think that is what Jesus calls us to, as Christians."

I do not address "you people," and I notice that I am not his people anymore.

## Kitchener 1997

Kaitlyn was in first year at Trent University in Peterborough when I got a phone call.

"Hi, mom, I have a friend on the rowing team, she is a lesbian.

Are you coming this weekend?

She would like to meet you. She doesn't know any old lesbians."

## Crosshill 1982

I had been the mother of two children when Benny Hinn came to Crosshill Mennonite Church as a part of the Abundant Life Conference, held at Bingeman Park in Kitchener every summer. Ron and I were very active with the conference and hosted some of the speakers at our home.

We did not host Benny Hinn. He did not get hosted, he was too big a name to be hosted, almost like the television evangelist. The conference was a big gathering, with lots of singing, dancing, and praying.

*Many years later, when I went to "witch camp" I was surprised at the similarities, not in the language used, but the fact that we sang, danced and chanted.*

I felt that if people really knew me they would not find me lovable or acceptable. When I went forward for prayer, Benny Hinn prayed over me and I was "slain in the spirit." I saw a bright light, and I heard a voice, they told me it was God's voice, telling me that I was perfect just the way I was. I wanted to believe it.

### Steinman's Church 1993

I told Fred I did not want to hide anymore and that I understood more now about what I was hiding from than I had when God had told me I was lovable in that moment of bright-light clarity at Crosshill Mennonite Church.

Fred told me that while it was probably okay for me to be a lesbian, "it was not okay," he said, "for me to act on it." I was unsure what that meant, and I tried to explain. This was our third meeting around the same topic. I was tired of these conversations. Fred was not the only person I was having them with. He was not the only person who felt it was their responsibility to remove the plank from my eye. I tried again to explain it was a world view, not only a sexual orientation but a world view. A woman-centric world view that I had always carried but been unable to identify or live out because of the patriarchal world that had me so entrenched. I explained again that, yes, it had to do with sexual attraction. But that it was so much more than that.

He said, "Sex is for procreation. Lesbian sex was never acceptable in the eyes of God because there could be no procreation."

"When," I wondered aloud, "when does sex happen? What is too much?" I asked, "is hand-holding sex?"

He said, "Probably not."

"When, then?" I persisted. "When does it become sex? Was a kiss alright?" I wondered. I was angry. I was tired of not being heard, of being preached at, of being told what my truth should be. Lashing out, I said, "Are you and Rosie still having sex? I hope you are preaching to your congregation that once the child-bearing years are past they should be no longer having sex." I said, "I am done talking to you about this."

He said, "I am sorry for how this conversation has gone."

I said, "I am glad it went this way, it was a good conversation for me!"

I walked out of his office, to my car in the church parking lot, and sobbed all the way home.

## *Mennonite Church North America 1993*

In the Mennonite Church, my cultural and spiritual home since my birth, you were not supposed to choose to be in a relationship with someone of the same sex. You were not supposed to be in relationship with someone of the same sex, no matter what. Those who lived in open relationship with someone of the same sex opened themselves to a forum for public discussion.

If we were going to be accepted or maybe even welcomed or maybe even able to play a role in the church, we needed to explain

> why we loved each other
> how we knew we loved each other
> how we knew God loved us

how we could justify our lives
how we understood some of the Levitican laws
whether we understood how difficult it was for
    people to see us
why we needed to flaunt

## Brunner 1992

My sister-in-law is told about my marriage with Ron ending before we have a chance to share with her. The Mennonite world I am a part of has a very successful network of rapid communication. An influential minister who was told in confidence shares with her. He shares with the world. He tells me I am a good Mennonite.

> He says, "You are respected in the church, you are on the Family Life Committee, you are a leader." He says, "You will give a positive face to lesbian and gay people."
>
> I say, "I am not coming out to be a spokesperson for lesbian and gay people in the church. I am not ready to come out publicly. I am grieving, I need time, divorce is difficult enough."

He shares my story.

He does not know my story.

He shares with others, who share with others, who share with others, that Ron and my marriage is over because I am lesbian.

I have left Ron.

I am attracted to women.

But.

I have not left Ron because I am lesbian.

Or because I am attracted to women.

## *Michigan 1998*

The Leaven Center in Michigan becomes a sacred land, a safe place to me in these days of ferment at home. I am seen and heard as I sit by the water and write, as I attend workshops, as I share my story and listen to other stories of pain, spiritual awakening and challenge. I feel affirmed and whole, even in my grief.

The eagle soaring overhead as we sing with Carolyn McDade, the tears that flow with the Grand River, as we share stories of rejection by churches and families we have believed we belonged to, offer hope in times of despair.

I am at home with nature's affirmation.

## *Twin Brooks Farm 1960*

At the end of the bush lane, which ran along the one brook of Twin Brooks Farm, lay the woods. I was in the woods. They were filled with life, the old hollow tree, a home I did not mind sharing during childhood, was a sacred haven. Buttercups, trilliums and jack in the pulpits, some of whom I was certain were janes, were my companions. Sometimes I was lucky and saw the owl, which on other days I only heard or imagined. Mink, otter, and muskrats swam in the water and fox and groundhog holes riddled the hills, along with arrowheads, some of which became part of treasured collections.

The hills and woods in the late 1950's often called me away from the house. Away from the baking, the cleaning, the laundry and the many other chores that were required of grandmother, mother and daughter on a busy mixed dairy farm. We did not feed the birds at Twin Brooks farm, there were plenty of seeds in the trees and scattered on the ground, throughout the fields, the garden and the yard. The mulberry tree outside my window was a favourite spot for birds and girls alike.

Brenda and I were cousins, born 6 months apart in the same hospital, our mothers were sisters-in-law. My mother loved her big brother, my uncle Earl.

Brenda and I learned early how to walk or bike the mile between our houses. It was less than a quarter mile for me to the corner where the one-room schoolhouse stood, then I turned right to head down the Schlegel Road, to what I learned early in life was the Schlegel homestead where Brenda lived.

Elaine, born 6 months after me, was my cousin too. She lived just up the road with my mom's only sister, Reta. Mom and Reta talked on the party line every day.

### Twin Brooks Farm 1962

Brenda and Elaine both rode our pony Betsy with me. But they were not there on the day Betsy came.

We were so excited, Dale and Bruce and I.

"Stop running around like a chicken with its head cut off," Dad yelled again, but I was too busy thinking about the chickens that had been butchered just the other day to really pay attention. They ran around much faster and more erratically than my brothers and I.

I wondered, why did Dad always have to yell so much? It was his fault we were excited. He was the one who brought Betsy home from the auction yard.

But as his voice got louder, I got slower and so did Dale and Bruce. It was important to slow down sometimes, even when you were excited, especially if Dad said so. Can we ride it? We asked. Dad said we could and Mom said, "Well it is not good for anything else."

Dad put a bit in Betsy's mouth and held on tight. Dale was the oldest so he got to ride first. Betsy went so slow, Dad leading her, almost pulling her to the end of the boulevard, when he turned to come back Betsy pulled away, and started trotting.

Now it was my turn, I swung my legs over her low back, grabbed the reins and said with great bravado, "It's okay, I can ride alone." Dad let go and said be careful. He didn't say I couldn't ride because I was a girl or anything, I was relieved. Betsy went slowly around the boulevard and when we got to the corner, she went faster. I was ready to go again and faster, but Dad said we had to let Betsy rest. She was not a young pony, he said. That's why she was such a deal.

Mom just shook her head. She did not make dad take Betsy back.

### Twin Brooks Farm 1959

My house was closer to the school than Brenda's, that is why the teachers all boarded at our house. Miss Newton was not my teacher, I was only four-years-old when she lived with us. Dale got to go to school with her, she got to be Dale's teacher. I thought Dale was lucky, being in her class.

Miss Newton was the only woman I knew who wore pants.

She wore plaid pants.

No women at our church wore pants.

She came from Toronto.

Sometimes her boyfriend Jim came to visit. They laughed a lot and had fun. One time they were playing, bouncing on the bed and they broke it. Mother was very angry. She was angrier than she ever got when we bounced on the bed.

Miss Newton moved out. I was sad and confused, but no one could answer my questions.

Mrs Magillaway, who then came to live with us, was not as much fun as Miss Newton.

### *Twin Brooks Farm 1964*

Brenda and Elaine and I spend hours in or under the shading mulberry tree, sharing the sweet succulence of mulberries. They fall on us, surround us. Sometimes our dresses and our underwear are stained purple. My aunt Florence gets angry when that happens.

Brenda and Elaine are family, I wish they were my sisters. I think they are lucky to have sisters. I like the map in Brenda's house. A map with pins all around the world, the pins are where the missionaries are. I like the flowers in Elaine's house, I like the sunporch and the kitchen smells.

Brenda and Elaine go to church.

I go to church. Our families go to church.

Church is the life I know and accept as the right life. It is at church that people are always pleasant with one another. There is lots of great singing in four-part harmony. Everyone is important and welcome at church, from the fresh air kids who come in the summer to spend vacation on the farm, to the Indians who come and live with families to go to school, to the foster kids. Everyone is welcome. Church is a safe place. Our minister comes to our barn to buy milk. He often comes at chore time, and then there is no fighting. I love when our minister comes at chore time.

### *Collingwood 2011*

Aunt Reta asked me, "Are the girls coming to the reunion?"

I said no I didn't think that Lisa would come or Lora ..."

She interrupted, "No not those girls, I mean Susan and Liw."

I hesitated. "Well, maybe Liw will, but I don't think Susan..." Looking at me with stern eyes, she replied, "They are your family, they are our family now, they both should come."

### *Kitchener 2003*

I missed the social justice community that the church provided so I sent out an email to friends and acquaintances and asked if they would like to be a part of a private refugee sponsorship.

Nine months after the email was sent out, nine months after people sent money, offered housing, met in groups to plan and share hopes and excitements, Flighte and her son Isaac arrived. She was welcomed at the airport by a community of women, many of whom were in loving relationship with other women.

When I held Issac in my arms in the airport for the first time he was five months old. It did not take long for Isaac and Flighte to become part of our family.

It took a few months before I was calling Flighte my daughter and I was her Canadian mother. She shared with me that if she had known it was a community of women who would be supporting her arrival in Canada, her mother would have made us all "clothes."

I am honoured to be given a gomeshi to wear at Flighte and Joshua's wedding.

## Twin Brooks Farm

I always knew it was important to accept people who were different. To show them the love that Jesus had for us. It was important to be kind and welcoming. My mother always welcomed people in our home. She said we might be welcoming angels unaware. Barney Fober used to visit my home, he used to ride the rails that ran along the back of farm, just behind the fields with the valleys and the arrowheads.

We called him a tramp.

My mother said we needed to be kind to Barney.

I was always excited when Barney came to visit, he would walk up from the back of the farm where I think he jumped off the train and show up at the kitchen door.

My mother would invite him in. He would not. My mother would offer him food, he would sometimes take the food and go outside and eat it.

Sometimes Barney would tell me where he had been. Most often Barney would take a hot drink from Mom and head out to the hay loft where he would spend the night.

Mom said we were not supposed to bother him.

I wondered, was he an angel?

Mom said that whatever you do to others, you are doing to Jesus too. Dad agreed with Mom, I think. I know that line is in the Bible.

## *East Zorra Mennonite Church 1969*

I knew that I needed to get to know Jesus as my personal Savior. I knew I had to invite him into my heart. I heard, "Just as I am without one plea" sung as people walked to the front of the church or tent, during tent meetings. I have heard that song since I was an infant.

Altar calls were not strange to me.

I went up at many altar calls. I was confident that if I got saved often enough I would be good enough. Soon I thought, it would happen.

It was after the altar call at the television evangelist Rex Humbard's crusade in Woodstock that I went to the minister and said I wanted to be baptized and join the Church. This was a big step. It meant that I was saved, that I was not going to hell. Surely, I thought, that meant I belonged, that I was good enough.

I was fourteen years old.

Baptism was a time of great celebration. After we were baptized we girls wore head coverings (small nets) to church (our grandmothers wore them all the time, some of our mothers did too). First Corinthians 11:6 says that if a woman does not cover her head she might as well cut off all her hair, or have her head shaved. I had long braids with ringlets when I was small, when I got baptized I still had long hair, but it was not in braids. My mother wore her hair in a French roll, which was a very fancy way of wearing long hair, it was not a traditional bun.

Some people criticized her for her French roll.

Verse 7 of 1st Corinthians says a man shall not cover his head for he is the image and glory of God, but the woman is the glory of man. I did not believe it was true that women should be submissive to men, I did not believe the head covering was relevant anymore, I believed that times were different now than in biblical times and that context should be examined.

I stopped wearing my head covering when I was dating Ron. Ron said he did not have a problem with me not wearing it. I was relieved. There were lots of other girls who did not think you needed to wear coverings either. The first Sunday I went to Ron's church, Crosshill Mennonite Church, I was confident I would not be the only girl not wearing a head covering, I knew others there who felt the same as I.

By the time I realized that all the other girls were wearing their coverings in spite of what they had told me, it was too late, the hushed whispers had started. And there I was with my naked head sitting in the pew.

### *Kitchener 1994*

My oldest daughter Lora is 16 when she decides she wants to be baptized. She has written a statement of faith in her religious studies class at school. She says she wants to be baptized by two ministers in two churches. She wants Anna from Olive Branch and Harold from Milverton to baptize her at Hidden Acres Mennonite camp where she has spent many happy hours as a lifeguard, a counselor and a camper.

People from Olive Branch tell her that she needs to commit to one faith community not two. She is told by people from Milverton that they cannot attend or celebrate with a community that condones same-sex relationship.

Both communities are important, Lora insists, both communities support her spiritual growth in different ways. If they will not come together to baptize her, she will not be baptized.

She is baptized with her mother and father and sisters and Anna and Harold and members of both churches in attendance and she shares with me that she is afraid that she will never be able to have a role in church leadership because of who her mother is.

I want to be a different mother, I am so proud of this daughter's standing strong on her ground. I wonder what would have happened if I had been able to do this earlier in my own life. Perhaps I would not have hurt her and her sisters so much. There are so many what ifs.

## Waterloo 2005

I lie on the bed, the sun streams in the window of Liw's and my home on Albert Street. We are having lots of conversations these days. We agree that I will call Carter. We trust Carter. She was a support to me through difficult times when I was on the CLOUT (Christian Lesbians Out) board. She is a friend who lives too far away, it is true, but a trustworthy and non-judgmental friend. She lives what she writes and teaches. Her book *Touching our Strength* was a support to me long before I knew its author. So I dial her number.

"Hi Carter," I say. "I have not talked to you for a long time."

"Yes," she says, it has been a long time. "Why are you calling?"

"Oh, I say," hoping for a little small talk first, "just missing you and wanted to chat."

"No," she says, "what's up?"

She knows me. I take a deep breath, and another. "Liw and I are thinking of opening our relationship. We are thinking of including someone else. Her name is Susan. I don't think you have met her. What are your thoughts?" I ask.

"It will be hard work," she says. "Do you think you are up to it? How are you and Liw doing? How are you doing?" She knows me well. She has heard many of my struggles. She knows my history. "It will be hard work," she says, "and it will be worth it. How are your girls?" she asks. Now that I have told her the real reason for my call, it is time for catch up. After I hang up I pull out my marked-up copy of *Touching our Strength* and read Carter's words about love being a choice, a conversion to humanity. I reflect on the many times she offered support during our shared days with CLOUT ( Christian Lesbians OUT) She has always been supportive, and has been an advocate for relational self.

Of course, I think. Of course, she would support stepping more deeply into love. Liw and I cuddle on the bed, sharing hopes, dreams and visions for expanding our world and our love.

## Komoka 2007

Ken and Carol and I are sitting around their dining room table in their home near London, Ontario. The tulips are in bloom in the backyard, and the redwing blackbirds have returned to the pond.

Ken asks, "Why aren't you coming out about Susan being a full, and equal partner of Liw and yours? You have always lived out loud," he says.

"I cannot put my girls through that again," I say. "I cannot put myself through that again. Judgment," I say, "is harsh. Not God's, God does not judge love. It is human judgment I fear."

I remind Ken as he pushes his glasses back on his nose that people told Lora that she should not support her mother, that because of who her mother was, she would never be able to be a Mennonite pastor, one of her long-term dreams. I remind him that, when Bonnie died, my daughters were told not to be sad because Bonnie had gone to hell and their mother would, too.

"Kaitlyn," I say, "lives in the Mennonite ghetto of Waterloo County, people talk and yes, people judge."

I am on a roll now, Ken gets to listen once more to my wounded heart.

> I am not willing to risk not having a relationship with my daughters. I am afraid, I am excited, I am alive. I want him to understand, I have been reading poetry, poetry is my solace, Adrienne Rich helps me understand when she says, "What we see, we see and seeing is changing." I tell Ken this, a grin spreads across his face.
>
> I say, "Liw and I are sharing our life and our love with Susan." I say, "I will name our love with people who also name and fully share their love and life with us."
>
> I am no longer interested in being an exhibit.
>
> "This is not," I say, "about changing the world."
>
> "This is," I say, "about living life out of love not out of fear."

This is about recognizing the expansiveness of love. No, I am not keeping secrets. I have determined, with the support of others, that there is a difference between holding things private and having secrets which erode the soul."

I am no longer interested in justifying my life. I am interested in living my life.


### Kitchener 1996

It has been over ten years since I read, *When Bad Things Happen to Good People*. Still I was arguing with the author, Rabbi Kushner.

Bonnie is suffering.

I am suffering.

I want the suffering to stop.

I want her suffering to stop.

I want my suffering to stop.

I do not want her to die.

I want her to die.

I want it to be over.

I want this waking up and rushing to the hospital to be over.

I do not care that Bonnie is accepting.

I am not accepting. I do not want her to be accepting anymore.

I do not think I am being punished for loving a woman.

I do not think that I am being punished for breaking my marital vows.

I am not happy that Bonnie tells me this is a great opportunity for me to really claim this wonderful life of mine. To take chances on love, to learn from the life she/we lived.

I love Bonnie.

> I am so angry when she says, "I have done what I came to earth to do, I came to love and be loved. And you," she says, "you taught me what it means what it really means to love and be loved."
> I am angry, I do not want her to be so accepting.
> I do not want to learn from her death to live my life.
> I do not think I am being punished by God.

*Kitchener 1993*

I am angry that people ask my daughters questions about my life. It is my life, questions that need to be asked, should be asked of me.

I am angry that my daughter is called a Lezzie at school because I am her mother.

I am angry that someone dares to pray for deliverance for my daughter because I am her mother.

I am angry that my daughters suffer at the hands of good Christians who believe that Lora, Lisa and Kaitlyn need salvation from me.


*Kitchener 1992*

I receive a phone call from our neighbour, our friend, in which she says she cannot participate in Bonnie's funeral. She has been at healing circles for Bonnie at our home, she has brought food, she has been a good neighbour.

She is a Mennonite minister I have trusted. She has spoken to another Mennonite minister who knows me, and who I thought supported me. He said if there were Mennonites at the funeral, if she participated, it might not look good,

It might be too pagan.

It might be too alternative.

Smoke rises from my ears. I make phone calls.

I am shocked when another Mennonite neighbour says he understands the Mennonite minister, who is our neighbour, who I thought was our friend, says he understands her decision to not participate in Bonnie's celebration of life.

My beloved is dying.

Bonnie and I do have friends, we have allies. Bob and Alan hear my tears, they are their tears too. Many other members of BMC (Brethern Mennonite Council for gay, lesbian and bisexual concerns), understanding friends, including Ruth and Lynn and Margaret and Hilda, hear me. They share my anger, my tears, my rage.

I have no rage left for the cancer. Our Mennonite minister neighbour gets all the rage, on behalf of all of the Mennonites whom I love and have loved. When she calls later and says she will, after all, play a role in Bonnie's celebration of life,

Bonnie tells me to tell her, "No. You are not needed."

When she calls to see if she can visit, Bonnie tells me to say "No."

When she calls to ask if it would be okay if she attends Bonnie's service, I say

"It is an open service, anyone who wants to is able to attend."

She says she will be there.

She is one of the 450 people who attend Bonnie's celebration of life.

She is one of the Mennonites who come.

### Kitchener 1993

I grieve, and I fear for my daughters who are affected by my life's call to live in love. I worry about the harm my life causes them.

I rage when I hear about them being prayed over, for generational sin.

I feel the deep clouds of darkness when there are prayer meetings about me, praying for me without talking to me, held by people who no longer talk to me.

## Kitchener 1995

Melanie calls me from her home at the Leaven Center.

> I ask, "Where is God?" I say I do not believe anymore.
> I say it hurts too much to believe.
> She is quiet, calm.
>
> All those casseroles left in your freezer, the rides to the hospital, all the flowers, the cottages that you vacation at, the lunches, the offers to sit with Bonnie, to stay with you or your girls or take them to movies or skiing or ...
> God, she says, is in all of those.

I am, once again, hopeful and I recall my inability to respond when seven-year-old Kaitlyn said "But Mommy, doesn't the Bible say to love everybody?"

## East Zorra Church 1970

Church was often a good place for me, a safe haven, a distraction from the turmoil within and without. I felt at home with the music, and with the people. I knew them and many of them knew parts of me, and yet I did not feel at home in my own skin. I felt, if these people knew me, really knew me, they would not like me.

## Twin Brooks Farm 1957

When my grandfather died I was almost three. I knew that I had wished that he was dead. I loved my grandfather, and I wanted him dead, he loved me and played with me and he hurt me. I was sad that my mother went to the hospital after he died. I did not understand that she did not leave me, that she did not bring home another baby because she was angry at me.

I did not tell my mother. I did not tell my grandmother that I had killed my grandfather.


## East Zorra Church 1966

The preacher at church said we were all bad, we all needed to repent. We could never know, he said, whether we were acceptable to God. We would never know whether we would go to heaven. We needed to work hard.

I did not ask whether I worked hard enough, I worked hard. I worked hard to be good enough. I did not know if there was ever a good enough. I guessed that was because I did not love God enough, or did not trust him enough, because if I would have, I would not have wished that I was dead.

I did not want to be like my mother. She would grow deeply depressed and discouraged. When she was depressed, she would say things I did not want her to mean. I decided she did not really mean it when she said she wished we, or I, had never been born, that *it* is too hard.

I did not care if she wished I had been born or not, I yelled at her, "I did not ask to be born."

Then we would both cry and go to our rooms. When we came out it would all be okay again, at least sometimes. When I came out of my room and could not find her, I would be afraid, very afraid. I would look for her, I was afraid she had killed herself. I wished I was a better daughter. I wished she was glad I had been born. I knew that if I had not yelled, she would be happier.

I knew, I remembered, Grandma's story, of being afraid her own baby was going to die on the day I was born, giving birth to me. I knew that my mother almost bled to death when I was born.

I believed I'd started killing her the day I was born.

I did not want her to be dead, I did not want her to die. Oh, how I loved my mother.

I would be a better daughter, I promised myself, if only she was still alive, I would be better. I would try harder to make her happy.

On those dark days, when I found her, I would tell her I was sorry, I told her I loved her, I told her I would behave better. I would be good. I promised.

**Twin Brooks Farm 1969**

The day my grandmother died, I was 14 and ironing in the kitchen. It was before the kitchen was renovated and we still had an ironing board that dropped out of the light green wainscoting in the wall.

The phone rang, one long and one short. Aunt Reta's ring.

Ours was two long.

Aunt Reta and Mom had gone to the hospital, maybe with other uncles and aunts, I do not remember, but I know that Aunt Reta and Mom were there.

Grandma had been home from the hospital for a few days then had to go back, there was something wrong with her blood, my mother had told me.

I heard the phone ring again one long and one short until someone answered, maybe one of my cousins, Barbara Anne, Sharon or Elaine, I did not pick the phone up to listen in. I did not want to know that grandma was dead. I already knew it before the phone rang again, at least, the way I remember it, it rang again two longs, our ring, but now I wonder did it ring again or did Barbara Ann and Sharon and Elaine come over from the farm one up and across the road to tell us? Barbara Ann was one of my oldest cousins to live nearby. She and Carol, Brenda's sister, were the older cousins, Barbara Ann babysat sometimes. She might have come over, but was it before or after I knew that grandma died? I wish now I could remember.

It was hard to be strong when I learned that grandma died, I loved her and did not want her to be dead. I loved her. And I loved what she did for our home. I was glad the intercom to the barn could be turned off when there was fighting, so that Grandma did not hear it.

I liked when the intercom was off.

I was strong and very sad after Grandma died. The casket did not come to our house like it had when Grandpa died.

When Grandpa died, I liked that my cousins, especially Elaine and Brenda, came and played in our yard. I sometimes hid behind the big fern, when there was no one to play with, and watched the casket.

I was 33 before I said to my mother, "I had this strange memory when I was talking with my therapist."

"What memory?"

"I remembered grandpa sexually touching me." I hurried to say, "It's crazy. I was little when he died."

"I knew," she said, "I knew I should never have left you alone with him."

Grandma's casket was in Krug's Funeral Home in Tavistock, at the front of the house where Bob Krug, the undertaker and his family, lived in.

I was not strong when I saw the casket with Grandma's body in it. I sobbed.

I was so surprised when Aunt Ruth and her silver-blue hair came over to me and put her arm around me. She sat beside me and rubbed my back. I was not afraid of Aunt Ruth when she rubbed my back, her fancy hair and clothes did not seem to make her different. She did not seem as different as my Mom and my Aunt Reta. I felt comforted by Aunt Ruth.

## East Zorra Mennonite Church 1969

Grandma died, but I still I sang soprano. Fred and Brenda sang in the choir with me.

All 40 youth members of the choir were part of the youth group of either Cassel, Hillcrest, East Zorra or Tavistock Mennonite church. Every Monday night we met to sing.

We plan to go hiking at choir practice at the end of September. There will be no choir next week. It is Thanksgiving weekend. We will go to the Thanksgiving service on Monday morning and we will leave from there to go hiking. The colours will be beautiful, we will go to the Bruce Trail entrance off Highway 6, near Dundas.

*Kitchener 1992*

It's when I am moving from my Brunner four-bedroom house into my basement apartment that I notice the fall colours, as if for the first time. I think they have never been more beautiful.

I hear from my brother Bruce, that Mom thinks, "I am not moving up in the world." By moving into a basement apartment. I do not hear this from Mom.

I think about how Mom would also think the colours are beautiful.

We disagree about so much these days.

*Brunner 1991*

I am sitting at my kitchen table, I have served the tea, and the muffins.

> I hear him say, "You are an abomination.
> The things I am hearing about you," he said, "are sinful."

I look at him, this elder at the church.

Ron has invited him to visit.

I look at Ron, he is silent. "What are you hearing?" I ask. Had someone seen me at a women's concert, with my non-Mennonite friends, with lesbians? I wonder.

Neither man says a thing.

I had spoken to Ron about my attraction to women.

I had spoken to two close friends at church in confidence.

I had not "acted" lesbian. Or had I?

Ron told me he would support me.

"We will figure this out together," he said.

Now, he remains silent.

The day before that, at church, we sang, "God's love is deeper than the deepest ocean, wider than the sky ... and there is nothing in this world that will ever change God's love." We sang together as we followed the words on the screen in the front of the hall.

I talked to our minister, Harold, after church. I told him I had a lesbian friend, Cheryl, who had grown up in the Pentecostal church and was going to come to church with me. She had been suspended from a Christian college because of her attraction to women. She no longer felt safe in the Christian world. I told her she would be welcomed at my church.

Harold looked at me, "Oh, Gloria," he said, "not now. We are dealing with too many other things right now. Don't bring her now."

## Stratford General Hospital 1990

I met Cheryl after she walked into the staff room after the meeting had begun. She was wearing white jeans and a red-plaid shirt, a bandana was looped around her neck. She looked like a cowgirl from my childhood fantasies of living on a big ranch with horses on the plains, some place where you could ride away into the sunset. Her grey hair sparkled as the autumn sun streamed into the window.

I felt alive.

The staff meeting ended. She came up, held out her hand.

"Hi," she said. "You must be Gloria. I am Cheryl. I live with Linda, she has told me so much about you."

I could be attracted to women. I was attracted to this woman. Why now? Why her? My mind raced with understanding, with confusion. All these years of being afraid of what people would think if they really knew me ... all these years of being afraid of what was wrong with me ... all these years.

*Brunner 1992*

My bicycle wheels crunched on the gravel, bird songs surrounded me, the leaves were budding, the spirit of new birth was all around me. How long had I been riding? I slowed down to get my bearings and look at my watch. It was almost 6:30. I had wakened early again, the wheels had been turning for over an hour now.

I turned away from Stratford and towards home. It was soon time to get the girls up for school.

Tears had been released.

I was not alone.

*"All will be well again, I know."*

Julian of Norwich in her turret jail cell sang with me again,

*"Love, like the yellow daffodil is coming through the snow ... all will be well again I know."*

My tired legs carry me upstairs to the girls' bedrooms. "Good morning, Good morning, Good morning ..." I sing as they open their eyes. "It's a beautiful day in the neighbourhood," I sing. Lora, Lisa and Kaitlyn groan as if in unison.

My interpretations of the Bible, my understandings of faith were growing, were changing. I was alive with discovery. I am so very confused.

I could not believe it when one of my closest friends from church told me that we could no longer be friends because we disagreed on basic tenets of the Bible.

I did not understand when I shared a book I found so helpful — *Between two Gardens* by James B Nelson, with two of my closest friends at church, that they would not talk to me about it, but would rather talk to each other about me.

I shared it with them because I thought it would help us understand and share deeply with one another, like we used to.

I am surprised, I am disappointed, when I ask one of them about it and she says

"Connie told me, "It goes against everything we believe, what else are you reading?'"

We had disagreed before. Surely we could disagree. Couldn't we?

It was hard not to call out to the people who crossed the street when they saw me coming towards them. I was shocked when the same people who used to say I had the gift of prophesy told me that I am channeling the Devil.

When Kaitlyn's friends, who had been part of her life and mine since their infancy, are no longer allowed to come to my house to play with her, I break.

Lisa sees my sorrow, my pain. "Mommy," she says, "it would be a lot worse if you were dead."

I want to protect my daughters from my life.

I want to protect my mother.

*Collingwood 2010*

Lora is visiting from her home in Indiana. Her friend Justin is with us at the kitchen table. Suddenly, it seems, he looks at me and says, "Did you move to Collingwood, just to get away from the Mennonites?"

*Olive Branch Mennonite Church 1992*

Olive Branch did not have a paid minister, everyone was expected to take part in the various roles needed to have a vibrant church community. There were monthly potlucks, with people from differing faith and cultural traditions as well as different socioeconomic backgrounds. There was a requirement that the "traditional mennos" — those of us who had grown up on potluck dinners — bring additional food to make sure all were fed.

Bonnie's and my attendance at Olive Branch make one thing clear. There is a need for a discussion on what the gathered community believed about full inclusion of LGBT people. And so, conversations begin. And we, Bonnie and I, are at the centre of the conversations.

## *Provident Bookstore Waterloo 1990*

Cheryl invites me to a poetry reading. I am excited to attend a reading by a Mennonite poet at a local bookstore. My mother and I used to go to Provident when it was on King Street in Kitchener, it used to be a highlight of our trips to town. I am excited that someone understands my love of poetry, someone even shares my love of poetry.

We arrive at the bookstore. There are Mennonites at the book reading, Di Brandt is after all a Mennonite poet. Di Brandt dares to say things I only think, most of the time.

I long to sit and listen and listen and listen.

I leave the reading.


## *Kitchener 1992*

I began a private counseling practice in Kitchener, as the first and only "out" lesbian therapist in the city. When people marvel at my strength, living an "out" life, I am able to share many stories of choice being taken away from me.

I had not chosen to come out.

My therapy practice soon became focused on spirituality and sexuality, as many women and men were losing their faith and their communities because of their orientation.

I hear stories.

I am honoured by stories.

Stories of despair, because individuals have been shunned by family, by friends.

I hear stories of isolation, of people no longer feeling at home at church.

Oh, the stories I hear.

## *Cambridge Ontario 1991*

I walked into a gathering of women-in-relationships-with-men who were questioning their sexual orientation. I felt afraid. I had gone to a restaurant in Kitchener to meet Chris's friend Barbara, who knew of a support group that was forming.

I told Ron where I was going.

He said, "It will be good for you to go. You need to sort yourself out. Maybe this will help you."

I drove the half hour from Brunner to Kitchener, listening to Meg and Cris at Carnegie Hall over and over again. Cheryl had given me this cassette, a welcomed introduction to women's music. "Song of the Soul" blaring from my cassette player drowned out the fear, the rock on my chest, as I thought about the women I was going to meet, women who were highly educated, from educated families. Different from me. I was just a confused rural Mennonite farmer's daughter and a farm implement dealer's wife.

Barbara, who I knew was a doctor, greeted me with a warm smile, her curly bob bouncing as we headed to the car. She soon let me know that she shared my anxiety about the gathering. She knew two of the other women who would be there, and was supportive of me and what she called my "courage" to attend this group of complete strangers.

I feel desperate, not courageous.

I needed to find answers, I needed support on this path I was on, and my selection of people who shared my life experience was very small. You could say it was non-existent.

Lesbians? What lesbians? I did not know lesbians!

I left my car in the parking lot of the mall on University Ave. and rode with Barbara to Cambridge, another half hour away where we walked into a beautiful century home. Apparently, the husband had gone out for the evening to allow his wife to host this gathering.

I looked at the faces of strangers.

Stories were exchanged, and it did not take long for me to understand that although this was not a Mennonite gathering, it was a gathering of kin of mine. There were single and partnered women, all who were in or had been in relationships with men, and were now questioning their orientation. Some, like me, believed that they could stay in marriages, with their newfound identities.

The most intimidating woman in attendance wore a flowing black dress and many silver necklaces. Bonnie was not a doctor or a nurse, she was studying social work. Her strength and determination shone through as she spoke and listened. She believed strongly in her right to live her life. She believed strongly that all women should live their lives.

I thought perhaps she was a witch. The thought intrigued and frightened. How could such a friendship support me as a Christian?

Over the months of our meetings, I learned that Bonnie did indeed practice pagan spirituality, although she did not call herself a witch. She had grown up in the United Church, and raised her children in it. She was now learning a variety of energy healing techniques and had no place for Christianity in her life. She felt the church was patriarchal, dominating. She did not want her daughter to grow up thinking she could not do anything and everything a man could do.

I shared that belief.

We had many lively discussions about feminist Christian possibilities, which I had been reading about voraciously for some time now. I argued often with her about paganism, saying that at least Christianity had a basis on which it was founded, Jesus. What, I would ask, is the basis of your paganism?

She was not afraid of my arguments and I became less afraid of her.

Bonnie continued to date men and to sort out what it meant to be bisexual in a world of either/or paradigms.

One of the women talked about first discovering her sexuality as a three year old, masturbating in the bath tub. "Wow," I said, just "wow." My life had been so different.

## Waterloo 1992

The spring rain is falling lightly. My tears are no longer contained when I see Bonnie's blue eyes link with my brown ones.

"What happened?"

This letter was from another friend of my youth, someone I had not had contact with for some time. Why did she think she had a right to tell me how I should be living my life? This letter, handwritten on pretty floral stationary meant, I assume, for friendly correspondence, explained it all. She had once been in a relationship with a woman, and had been saved from her sinful ways. I could be too if I only repented. The letter was four pages long. "Call me," the letter said, a phone number followed. "Call me and I will help you leave your sinful lifestyle." She gave other options, there were change ministries aplenty.

Bonnie began to sing a song composed by Alaskan singer/songwriter Libby Roderick:

> *How could anyone ever tell you*
> *you were anything less than beautiful?*
> *How could anyone ever tell you*
> *you were less than whole?*
> *How could anyone fail to notice*
> *that your loving is a miracle?*
> *How deeply you're connected to my soul.*

## Kitchener 1992

Six months after the tears in Bonnie's living room, the furniture was all in place, the bunk beds and futon installed in this bedroom, decorated with mother love. The apartment smudged and blessed, was now ready for Lora, Lisa and Kaitlyn's first overnight in what I hoped would soon be their second home.

Bonnie sent a bouquet of flowers, support from Seattle.

Bonnie and I bought a home together and moved in, filled with hope, on her 50th birthday, October 24, 1993.

*Kitchener 1995*

A little more than one year and one cancer diagnosis later, I eagerly open a Christmas card whose return address is an old friend I had not heard from since my divorce. I believe in the bonds of friendship we had shared since high school.

I read, below the Merry Christmas wish, that the devil has me by a fish hook and unless I repent from the life I am living, I and the woman I live with will burn in hell's fires.


*Kitchener 1996*

Easter Sunday. Bonnie's mother, Bonnie's aunt, Bonnie's daughter and her boyfriend, Bonnie's sons and her grandson, Bonnie's brother and his wife sat in the room where Bonnie lay asleep, while we laid with her, sat beside her, while we held her hand.

We are all afraid to celebrate Easter, we cannot celebrate new life. On this Easter Sunday I have willingly agreed to Lora, Lisa and Kaitlyn going with their dad.

Bonnie's eyes are closed, her breathing laboured.

She opens her eyes. The men go to the living room. The women hold vigil. The men come in and out. Friends come in and out. I am in and out. We speak sometimes quietly, sometimes laughing. Mostly we sit, together and alone, we sit.

On Monday morning Bonnie opens her eyes and looks at me. "Never again," she says, "never again will you allow that many people into this room to sit and wait for me to die. You were all, they were all," she emphasizes, "just waiting for me to die."

My words, my explanations, are rejected.

I return from a reluctant lunch with Lou and Karrie that Monday, my mother is upstairs cleaning. Bonnie looks at me from her bed in the sunlit and flower-filled room and says, "You are never here anymore."

I know she will soon be gone. I know she will soon die. Then she says, "Your mother and I worked everything out."

"You did?" I ask.

"Yes," she smiles, "it is all okay."

"What did she say?"

"None of your business. It was our conversation," she laughed.

In that moment, I hoped she would live forever.

### *Pandora Street Kitchener 1996*

When my mother walked into the kitchen, the snow was melting, slowly, the trees were just beginning to bud. She handed me the laundry basket filled with neatly ironed clothes. I had no time for ironing in a life of chemotherapy and hospital visits, there was barely enough time for attending daughters' school and extra-curricular events.

There, on top of the laundry basket, was a neatly folded purple lace teddy. My mother had found some clothing from before the days of despair in the pile I'd given her to iron.

There it was, the purple teddy, displayed on top.

Perhaps another life was possible.

Four months after the fish-hook Christmas card arrived I felt Bonnie being torn from me. I saw her being led out the window by angels. Angels had been regular visitors, since her spirit guide Jesus became her companion.

My mother returned with a pot of soup, and worried eyes.

*Tavistock 1997*

We — my mother, father, Liw and I — sit around the kitchen table. As the snow piles around us, my mother places the cheese and fruit bread in the middle of the table. My mother has made tea. Bonnie has been dead for nine months. Liw sits on one side of the table. My father sits on the end, opposite my mother. It is quiet, so very quiet.

My sentence breaks the silence, "Liw and I are going to have a commitment celebration."

"What is that?" asks my father.

"It is like a wedding," I reply.

His intake of breath is audible.

My mother speaks quietly, "Oh, Gloria, it is too soon, Bonnie has not been gone very long, take time."

I agree with my mother, it is sooner than I had anticipated, it is sooner than I'd thought. I knew others who would feel the same way, say the same thing.

And I said, it was right, I was certain.

I could not turn away from this gift of love.

Liw was quiet.

My mother said, "We like you Liw, it is not about you."

My father slammed his hand on the table. "It is not right," he said "The Bible …"

I cut him off.

"We will not come," my father said.

"I do not want you to come if you cannot celebrate with us. It would be wonderful if you could celebrate with us, but if you cannot …."

"I love you," my mother said.

"I know," was my reply, "Your attendance or not does not change your love for me, I know that." Tears run down my cheeks. I rise and leave the table. I return to silence.

My mother, crying softly, passes the bread and cheese. More tea, she offers us more tea.

There will be no card games played around this table today.


*Tobermory 1996*

Lynn and I travelled up and down the Tobermory streets, on our day trip from the cottage on Johnson Harbour that Jane and Carol continued to offer with generous caring spirits. We looked in rock shops. I love rock shops. I love the magic the possibility.

I have already met Liw, it is only five months since Bonnie died. I do not know if it is ok to love again, so soon. I am conflicted. Lynn and I talk of sharing rocking chairs in old age. We talk about the gift of love, she is irritated that she has had to "kiss so many frogs" and I have already met a potential partner, a potential soul mate. We wander into another shop.

A fossil hangs on a black cord string.

Look I say, it is about the journey of life, we are all fossils becoming.

It is a moment of sacred awareness.

I turn and walk out of the store.

Lynn meets me on the sidewalk.

You too are valued she says, as she hangs the cord around my neck.

## *2004*

I worked for the Supportive Communities Network (SCN) of the Brethren and Mennonite Council for Gay, Lesbian, Bisexual and Transgender (BMC) concerns. I attended national church conferences. I travelled across Canada and the United States to visit churches, to encourage dialogue and to support churches in becoming publicly welcoming to LGBTQ people.

I met many wonderful people on my travels and had many great conversations with people who saw love as a primary Jesus message and who believed that the church was a place for all.

During the time that I worked for this supportive network, my awareness of the power of love over fear grew. I spent time with a community of others, singing in the halls, outside the gates of conference centres, wearing brightly coloured rainbow shirts, and reading placards carried by protesters that said "God hates sinners." I understood that meant God hated me.

The fear that I experience surprises me.

Lora, Lisa and Kaitlyn are reminders that I do have something to live for. Their resilient spirits fill me with hope.

The fear that I became aware of within the leaders in the church that I called my home, I found unfathomable. How could those of us who believed in faith, who followed a God of love, be led by leaders who feared their own members? I met with church leader after church leader who told me, in different and the same words, that the church was not ready yet, that they did not want a church split, that I/we needed to be patient.

Over and over again, I heard fear about what would happen to the church if it became more accepting, if it became more open to diversity, if it was welcoming to all regardless of sexual orientation.

I heard over and over and over again that I was dispensable, I was collateral damage.

This could not be my church, this was not my understanding of divine love.

This was not my home. Perhaps Nelle Morton was right, perhaps *the journey is home*, and the journey continues.

*My* spiritual home was inclusive, welcoming to all, an earth mother holding her child.

Before I moved into a room of my own, before I prepared the apartment for my girls, as the sun shone brightly and I house-sat for friends, as I tried to care for my children, as I lived with contradictory hope and despair, before all that, I tried to negotiate with God.

I argued.

I pleaded.

I told Him I would fight for lesbian, gay, bisexual and transgendered rights in the church.

I told Him that I would speak out more confidently, louder, on behalf of the oppressed if S/He would just let me stay in my marriage, and not make me go public.

I felt like Jonah, called to another land I did not know, not to condemn, but to assure them of God's love, and at the same time, claim the preciousness of God's love for me. I wondered when the whale would come to swallow me.

*New York State 2014*

I am doing Mindful Self Compassion teacher training with a small group in upstate New York. Where we are asked to share our experiences of a shame exercise and practice our inquiry skills with one another. I wait until there is no one left. My strong need to please and to be acceptable pushes me to agree to be the person being questioned. Rosemary, from Melbourne Australia, and I have shared much this week, I trust her and yet my heart is closed. I am hurting. I do not want to talk about my shame again. It does not shift. It did not shift in California when I did the first Mindful Self Compassion training. I hurt my daughters so much by my decisions, I continue to feel shame. I know it is not going to shift now. I want to be a good group member. I know I do not belong to my community, yet I want to belong. How can I belong and live my truth? I want to cooperate and I want to live. I cannot choose not to live.

I watch as group members reach out to Rosemary, as inquiry after inquiry comes back to her. I could do nothing to help her.

The trainers move from group to group and this time, Christopher Germer, one of the MSC founders, who I admire, is in our group. After allowing Rosemary to work with me for what seemed to me to be an eternity, Christopher gently and quietly asks her and me, could he try something?

We give him permission to speak.

His blue eyes penetrate my brown ones as he asks, "Gloria, do you want to let go of the shame?"

The rush of monkey mind is great. In mini-seconds, I debate how I can possibly answer this without sounding like an imbecile. Of course I want to get rid of the shame, who wouldn't want to get rid of the shame, did he think I was stupid?

I answer a quiet, yes.

I do not know what he says as he continues. I cannot hear. Then I do. I hear him tell me that we all have a well of grief within us ... and the tears begin to flow, my tears, his tears, around the group, the well of tears begins to flow. I do not know exactly what happened next but I find myself in holding arms of love.

Lunch follows. I had prearranged a lunch meeting with Michelle, another beloved trainer, to talk about what to do with this stuck piece in my life, this piece of not belonging to a community I was longing for.

Michelle and I meet, sitting on a wooden bench overlooking the courtyard, filled with new friends from around the world. I share with her a little of the group experience of the previous hour. I am self-consciously aware that there are many people who would like to talk to Michelle. I tell her I probably don't even need to talk to her now, if there are others .... She cuts me off, telling me she would like to hear more of my story. So we sit on the benches, facing west, and chat. I hear a little about her family, her husband and boys, then I tell her more of my story.

She sits beside me. Leaning forward to hear me, she listens, is quietly present. I share about the cost to those I loved, especially my daughters, and to me, as I responded again and again to what I name as the persistent calls of God in the night, calls that remind me of Samuel in the Hebrew scriptures (1 Samuel 3). I am surprised to hear myself telling her my story of almost sixty years.

Michelle stops me, looks at me for a moment.

"What if it was not the cost of leaving the church, of leaving your community that has been so hard to bear? What," she asks, "what if the real cost was staying too long?"

*Collingwood 2015*

I head off to the Bed and Breakfast, three days by myself, a treat for sure. Three days of hiking, of writing, of being fed. A self-directed retreat. I am feeling almost giddy with delight. I will be alone with myself and my thoughts. I will sleep when I want, walk when I want, eat when and what I want.

This is what I do.

The breezes blow lightly through my hair as the leaves red, yellow and golden brown rustle below me. The hoot hoot as the evening setting sun reflects into my window, the distant sound of water winding its way along the stream offer me sweet solace as I sleep

I am gifted, by the delicious food of my hosts, the sausage with just enough garlic and the still lingering scent of pork loin takes me into the days of my youth with the eggs, with their farm fresh deep yellow yolks. I savour food, I savour savoury and sweet.

I savour life!

I had negotiated not to be in touch, with my beloved's to be in silence with myself.

As I head to bed on day three, I wonder what are Liw and Susan doing? Where are they? Are they missing me?

I am missing them.

I am almost asleep, dozing, when I awake with a flash.

I would be just fine if they left me, if they were to die.

I would grieve, I would be sad, I would grieve … and I know how to grieve and I know how to be sad, and I know how to live. I know how to love, and how to be loved.

I could live alone and be happy. I am whole as me.

I lay awake a long time. I laugh, I cry and I write.

## *Collingwood 2016*

The labyrinth is alive with red, purple and yellow tulips, a few daffodils still stand and the forget-me-nots are just beginning to show themselves not only here but throughout the yard. The dandelions, I know, in the midst of the dainty blue blooms, are good for the bees.

There is nothing that needs removing. There is nothing that needs pulling.

All is well.

*Acknowledgements*

My thanks to Susan Scott for editing, encouraging, editing, encouraging, editing, encouraging and believing in me and in friendship.

The organizers of National Novel Writing Month, and all those writers who cheered and encouraged me as I wrote the first 60,000 unedited words.

Thank you to all of you, whom I began to list and found the task impossible, there are so many of you, who have supported this project, and ME.

You know who you are!

You amazed me by reading through 60,000 words of run-on-sentences and gave detailed feedback, you read again and again, you listened as I read, you sent emails and cards, you encouraged me financially, emotionally, physically, and spiritually to claim my voice. You told me my story was important and needed to be told. You loved/love me.

My deepest gratitude to Michelle, Christopher and Kristen and my Mindful Self Compassion co-learners.

Many thanks to my family of birth and of choice, my children and grandchildren, and those who cheer me on from the other side Bonnie, Jerry, Mom, Harriet, Dad and Ron.

My love to Susan and Liw, words are insufficient.

Love is limitless.

www.ingramcontent.com/pod-product-compliance
Lightning Source LLC
Chambersburg PA
CBHW021449070526
44577CB00002B/331